Dreamtime
PAINTERS

Rob Waring, *Series Editor*

NATIONAL
GEOGRAPHIC
L E A R N I N G

Australia · Brazil · Mexico · Singapore · United Kingdom · United States

Words to Know

This story is set in Australia. It happens in the Kakadu (kạkədu) National Park. A **national park** is a special area where animals and nature are protected.

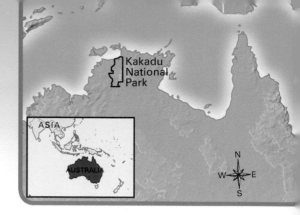

(A) **Animals in Australia.** Read the definitions. Write the number of the correct <u>underlined</u> word next to each item in the picture.

1. A <u>kangaroo</u> is an Australian animal that jumps on its back legs.
2. <u>Insects</u> are small living things with six legs; for example, beetles or spiders.
3. <u>Reptiles</u> are cold-blooded animals that lay eggs and have pieces of hard skin, or 'scales,' on their bodies.
4. A <u>turtle</u> is an animal with four legs and a hard back covering that lives mainly in water.
5. <u>Rock</u> is the hard, natural material that forms part of the earth.

The Australian Outback

B The Aboriginal Civilization. Read the paragraph. Then match each word with the correct definition.

The Aboriginal civilization is one of the world's most ancient civilizations. They have lived on Earth for at least forty thousand years. 'Dreamtime' is the Aboriginal story of how the world began. Aboriginal artists often paint pictures about the Dreamtime story. Aboriginal art is very beautiful and very valuable.

1. civilization _____
2. ancient _____
3. Earth _____
4. Dreamtime _____
5. artist _____
6. art _____

a. the world on which we live
b. someone who paints or draws
c. very old
d. the culture and society of a people
e. paintings and drawings
f. an Aboriginal name for the time
when the world began

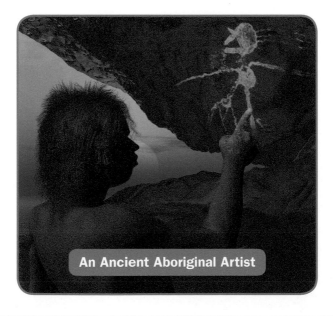

An Ancient Aboriginal Artist

Australia is a very large country with a varied landscape. It has **rain forests**,[1] the outback **desert**,[2] and the seaside. It also has a special warm area in the North. Here, you can find art that is over 30,000 years old! It is the rock art of the Dreamtime Painters.

---

[1] **rain forest:** an area with many trees and plants where it rains very often
[2] **desert:** an area, often covered with sand or rocks, that has very little water

🎧 CD 2, Track 05

Aboriginal rock art is ancient. It was around long before there were roads and towns. It was in Australia long before people from other countries arrived. It comes from a time when Aboriginal rock artists painted the 'Dreamtime.'

Dreamtime is an Aboriginal story about the beginning of the world. It describes a time long ago when rocks, animals, plants, and people first came to the earth. It's a big part of Aboriginal history and culture.

Aboriginal images of the Dreamtime can be seen in ancient rock paintings throughout Australia. There are large numbers of these paintings under the ground of Kakadu National Park; a park which is owned by the Aboriginal people.

Rock Paintings

Ancient Dreamtime Painters made many rock paintings long ago.

Thompson Yulidgirru[3] is an Aboriginal artist. He still paints in the traditional Aboriginal way. He tells how he learned the old Aboriginal stories from his grandfather. However, the stories go back much further than Thompson's grandfather. Thompson explains, "When I used to go stay with my grandfather, I used to tell him, 'Please...tell me the stories from my **ancestors**.[4]'"

Ian Morris is a **naturalist**[5] who has lived in Australia most of his life. He has studied these Dreamtime paintings, and feels they are very special. They are unlike any other paintings in the world. Morris explains; "They say that the rock art here goes back almost as far as any known civilization. They're the oldest art records of human civilization in the world."

---

[3]**Thompson Yulidgirru:** [tɒmpsən yulɪdʒəru]
[4]**ancestor:** member of a person's family from very long ago
[5]**naturalist:** person who studies plants, animals and nature

Predict

**Answer the questions. Then scan page 12
to check your answers.**

1. How long have the Aboriginal people lived
   in Australia?

2. Other than the Dreamtime, what kind of
   stories do the rock paintings tell?

The Aboriginal people have most likely lived in what is now Australia for at least forty thousand years. They may have even been here for as long as a hundred thousand years. This means that they are the oldest continuous human culture on Earth.

The ancient art of the Aboriginal people is like a history book. It's also a **guide**[6] to everyday life. Their pictures tell stories about birds that tell kangaroos when **hunters**[7] are approaching. The paintings also tell stories of war.

---

[6]**guide:** a list of helpful information
[7]**hunter:** a person or an animal that kills for food or sport

In the past, Aboriginal people believed that these paintings had special powers. They believed that if they painted a lot of **fish**,[8] they would catch a lot of fish. The **seasons**[9] of the year were significant to the Aboriginal people, as well. They only painted certain images at specific times of the year.

In addition, certain groups of Aboriginals only painted certain animals. If a group painted turtles, that's the only thing they painted. They didn't paint kangaroos as well. These ancient painters regarded their art as special. They thought it kept the earth strong and healthy.

---

[8]**fish:** a kind of animal that usually has scales and lives in water
[9]**season:** one of the four periods of the year; spring, summer, fall, or winter

However, things have changed nowadays. Most Aboriginal painters no longer paint on rock. In fact, the last real rock artists died in the 1960s. Today Aboriginal artists paint on **bark**,[10] paper, and wood. That way, they can carry their art everywhere and sell it easily.

Aboriginal art is getting more and more **famous**.[11] People everywhere want to buy Aboriginal art and prices are sometimes very high. One piece of Aboriginal art can now cost a lot of money, perhaps tens of thousands of Australian dollars.

---

[10] **bark:** the hard outer covering of a tree
[11] **famous:** known and recognized by many people

Fact Check: True or false?

1. There aren't any real rock artists today.

2. Artists now paint on paper and wood.

3. Aboriginal art does not cost very much.

Unfortunately there's now a problem with the original rock paintings. Many of them are losing their color due to time and bad weather. Insects and reptiles also walk over the paintings and make them lose their color. "There are all these **agents of deterioration**[12] acting on the art," reports Morris. "We can only slow that down [not stop it]." Fortunately, there is a lot of rock art in Australia, and they're finding more all the time.

Many Aboriginal people are trying to keep in contact with their history in modern times. The rock art of the Dreamtime Painters may just help them do this. Hopefully, these ancient paintings will help modern-day Aboriginal people understand the thoughts and ideas of their ancestors. Hopefully, they will help save the memories of the great civilization who owned this land long ago, and who still own it today.

---

[12] **agents of deterioration:** things that make the condition of something worse

After You Read

1. On page 4, what is the meaning of the word 'varied'?
   A. simple
   B. changing
   C. artistic
   D. beautiful

2. What is the best heading for page 7?
   A. Rock Art Shows Recent Aboriginal Stories
   B. Ancient Towns and Roads in Rock Painting
   C. Dreamtime Paintings Tell of Long Ago
   D. Aboriginal Music Tells Ancient Story

3. What did the artist Thompson Yulidgirru want his grandfather to teach him about?
   A. making rock art
   B. his family's history
   C. ways to paint
   D. Aboriginal beliefs

4. Naturalist Ian Morris thinks that Aboriginal rock art:
   A. is special to the world
   B. shows that Aboriginal civilization is modern
   C. was not painted by Aboriginal people
   D. all of the above

5. The Aboriginal people have the oldest _____ in the world.
   A. continuous human culture
   B. towns
   C. naturalists
   D. painter

6. On page 15, 'significant' means:
   A. hard
   B. wonderful
   C. important
   D. troubling

7. Why do Aboriginal artists paint on bark now?
   A. There are no more rocks.
   B. They like paper and wood.
   C. It's easier to paint on bark.
   D. People can buy and move bark paintings.

8. One piece of Aboriginal art can cost:
   A. hundreds of Australian dollars
   B. thousands of Australian dollars
   C. tens of thousands of Australian dollars
   D. hundreds of thousands of Australian dollars

9. In paragraph one on page 19, 'them' refers to:
   A. paintings
   B. insects
   C. artists
   D. reptiles

10. How can we stop the deterioration of the rock paintings?
    A. Brighten the colors.
    B. Kill insects and reptiles.
    C. Stop the bad weather.
    D. There is nothing we can do.

11. People are _____ finding Aboriginal rock art all the time.
    A. many
    B. still
    C. even
    D. ever

The LASCAUX PAINTINGS

Near the town of Montignac in Southern France, visitors can find some of the most beautiful cave paintings in the world—the Lascaux Paintings. The history of these paintings is very interesting. Caves are large rooms that have been formed by nature. Most caves are under the ground, but some have entrances that people can find. In September 1940, that's just what happened. Four boys were taking a walk in the woods near Montignac. As they walked along, one of them noticed an unusual rock. When they got closer, they realized that it wasn't a rock; it was an opening in the ground. This opening led to a cave. The boys decided to have a look around this cave. The walls of the cave were covered with ancient art. The boys didn't know it, but the cave was the find of the century!

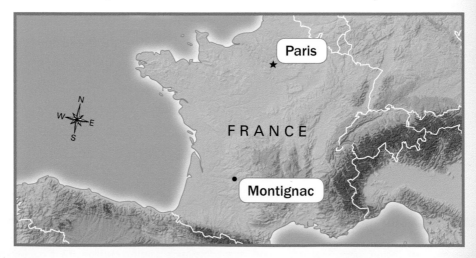

Some cave paintings show large groups of animals.

Over the years, many historians and artists came to study the art. They wanted to understand who painted them and what they might mean. They soon realized that some of the art indicated animals that were on Earth a long time ago. However, these animals no longer exist. Many of the pictures also showed people following animals and trying to kill them for food. In the end, historians agreed this was likely to be the art of a civilization that existed over 15,000 years ago.

By 1950, over a thousand people from all over the world were visiting the caves every day. But by 1955, the paintings were beginning to become difficult to see. Because so many people were passing through the caves, the paintings were losing their color. Sadly, people can no longer visit the caves. However, another set of cave paintings has been created. These paintings look exactly the same as the Lasaux Paintings. People made the paintings so that everyone can still learn about this ancient civilization. If you are near Montignac, these caves and wonderful paintings are a must-see!

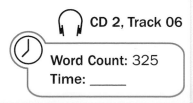

CD 2, Track 06

Word Count: 325
Time: _____

Vocabulary List

agents of deterioration (19)

ancestor (10, 19)

ancient (3, 7, 8, 12, 15, 19)

art (3, 4, 7, 10, 12, 15, 16, 19)

artist (3, 7, 10, 16)

bark (16)

civilization (3, 10, 19)

desert (4)

Dreamtime (3, 4, 7, 8, 9, 10, 19)

Earth (3, 7, 12, 15)

famous (16)

fish (15)

guide (12)

hunter (12)

insect (2, 19)

kangaroo (2, 12, 15)

national park (2, 8)

naturalist (10)

rainforest (4)

reptile (2, 19)

rock (2, 4, 7, 8, 9, 10, 16, 19)

season (15)

turtle (2, 15)